CONTENTS

THE CHARACTERS

Mary

God has chosen Mary to be the mother of his son. What will this mean for her?

Joseph

Engaged to Mary, Joseph too has responsibility for the young Jesus. What can he teach him?

Elizabeth and Zechariah

Elizabeth and Zechariah think they are too old to have children, until an angel visits Zechariah. Who will their son become?

Jesus

Jesus is the Son of God, but he is also Mary's son. How will the events of his life affect his mother?

John the Baptist

John is preparing the way for someone special – who is it?

Simon Peter

A loyal friend to Jesus. Can he help Mary through events no mother should experience?

Mary Magdalene

One of Jesus's closest friends. What experiences will she share with Jesus's mother?

5

MARY OF GALILEE

My son. Even now those words swell my aging
heart with love before wringing it with agony.
I want to shout his name from the rooftops;
I want to curl up tightly and weep. Oh, my son.

You've probably heard stories of his birth, his
life and his death. Can you spare the time to listen
to my account? I should like to tell the whole story,
just once, before I die. You needn't worry that the
swiftly-passing years might have diminished my
memory. How could incidents of such intensity ever
fade? Every day of my life I live with the physical
pain and motherly joy of the beginning, and with
the maternal agony and spiritual reward of the end.

I'm sure I'm not the only person to have wondered
why God chose me. I still wonder. I was an ordinary
Jewish girl from an ordinary, happy family.

My parents were good people who kept the Lord's commandments. We loved God, we loved each other, and we loved our life in the Galilean village of Nazareth. I also loved Joseph, a craftsman, who had recently asked me to marry him. As I said, ordinary. Nothing unusual.

Do you believe in angels? I think I had always believed in them, but that didn't make it any less of a shock when one appeared before me. I must have been about fourteen years old when it happened. I was alone in the house, sewing, when the quality of the light seemed to change. I squinted up from my close work. As my eyes gradually adjusted, I saw a man, or at least a being, all in white, suffused with the purest light you can imagine. You ask me how I felt? Afraid, of course.

The angel smiled. 'Do not be afraid. The Lord is with you.' I stared, transfixed. His voice was gentle. 'Mary, you have pleased God.

You will soon be with child. You will give birth to a son, and you will name him Jesus. He will be called the Son of the Most High, and his kingdom will never end.'

My mind span so quickly that I felt dizzy. 'How can this happen?' My voice must have been a terrified squeak. 'I am unmarried, a virgin.'

'The Holy Spirit will come upon you, and the power of the Most High will overshadow you, so the holy one to be born will be called the Son of God.'

'The Son of God?' I gasped.

The angel, who told me his name was Gabriel, hadn't finished. 'Your relative Elizabeth is also going to have a child,' he continued. 'She is already in her sixth month of pregnancy.'

I was astonished. Elizabeth had never been able to have children, and now she was an old woman.

'Nothing is impossible with God,' asserted Gabriel.

In spite of everything, I trusted his words. 'I am the Lord's servant,' I replied. 'May it be as you have said.'

My parents supported me. They suggested that I visit Elizabeth, who lived with her husband in the Judean hills. As I approached, I saw her outside her house and called out to her. Giving an astonished cry, she put her hands on her rounded belly. 'Mary!' She rushed towards me. 'Mary! As soon as I heard your voice the baby in my womb leapt with joy. Blessed are you among women, and blessed is the child you bear. Why am I so favoured that the mother of the Son of God should visit me?'

'How do you know I'm pregnant?' I asked in wonder. 'And how do you know who my baby is?'

Elizabeth led me inside. 'Sit down and rest,' she smiled. 'I'll explain.'

I looked at her kind, aging face, blooming with the promise of motherhood. 'I think it's you who should rest,' I said.

Elizabeth's husband, Zechariah, had followed us inside. He silently beckoned to us both to sit down, then went to prepare some drinks.

'I'm afraid Zechariah can't speak,' explained Elizabeth. 'An angel told him that he would not be able to speak again until our son is born.'

Zechariah came back into the room, and nodded ruefully. I sat forward in my seat. This story promised to be as strange as my own.

'Six months ago,' began Elizabeth, 'Zechariah was on duty in the temple. He had been chosen from amongst the other priests to go into the inner temple and burn incense.'

'How did he tell you this if he can't speak?'

'He wrote it down,' explained Elizabeth. 'Mary, did an angel visit you?' she asked me. I nodded. 'Then you'll be able to imagine how Zechariah felt when an angel appeared beside the altar.' I nodded again. 'The angel told him not to be afraid, that our years of prayer had been answered. He said that I would bear a son, and that we must call him John.' Elizabeth chuckled. 'I wish I could have seen Zechariah's face. The angel told him that God will love our son and fill him with the Holy Spirit.' Elizabeth's face had grown more serious. 'John is supposed to bring Jewish hearts back to God and bring disobedient people back to righteousness. He has to prepare our people for someone who is to follow.' She looked at my own belly, which was not yet showing signs of the child growing within it.

'But why can't Zechariah speak?' I asked.

'Poor man,' smiled Elizabeth. 'He angered the angel by asking him how he could be sure. "I am Gabriel," the angel scolded him. "God sent me to tell you this good news. Because you doubted God's words, you will be unable to speak until your son is born."'

Zechariah went to fetch our drinks. Placing them on the table, he indicated that we should all join hands, then he looked expectantly at me. The need to praise God bubbled within me, and the words erupted from me. 'My soul praises the Lord, and my spirit rejoices in God my saviour, for he has recognised our humble status. From now on all generations will call us blessed, for the mighty one has done great things for us. Holy is his name! His mercy extends to all those who fear him. He has performed mighty deeds, he has scattered those who are proud. He has brought down rulers from their thrones and has raised the humble. He has filled the hungry with food, but the rich he has sent away empty. He has helped our people, remembering to be merciful to the descendants of Abraham forever, just as he promised.'

I stayed with Elizabeth for three months, returning home just before her son was born. She later told me that Zechariah's voice didn't return immediately. On the day of John's circumcision, Elizabeth's neighbours said, 'You should call him Zechariah, after his father.'

'I'm not going to call him Zechariah,' Elizabeth replied.

'What do you want to call him?'

'John.'

'John?' they exclaimed. 'But you have no relatives called John! What about tradition?'

They called on Zechariah to name the baby, handing him a stone tablet to write upon. 'His name is John,' he wrote. Immediately, he was able to speak again. 'His name is John.'

Years later, Zechariah described having felt the same urge to praise God that I had experienced. 'Praise be to the Lord,' he remembered shouting, as soon as his voice returned. 'He has saved his people from our enemies and from the hand of all who hate us. He will show mercy and enable us to serve him without fear in holiness and righteousness forever.' Raising his new son towards heaven, he blessed him. 'You, my child, will be called a prophet of the most high; for you will prepare the way for the Lord. You will teach people that they will be saved by the forgiveness of their sins, because of the tender mercy of our God. The rising sun will come to us from heaven to shine on those living in darkness, to guide our feet into the path of peace.'

People wondered at this for many months. What was this baby going to do? Meanwhile John quietly began the job of growing up, until it was time for him to play his very important role.

As I said, I was engaged to be married to Joseph. Joseph was a good man and was quite understandably upset when I told him that I was pregnant. He knew without a doubt that he was not the father. How could he marry me? The angel Gabriel appeared to Joseph in a dream and explained everything. The wedding could go ahead as planned.

In the final month of my pregnancy, the emperor, Augustus, wanted to know how many people lived in the Roman world, and what property we owned. He therefore ordered a population census. Every man had to register himself and his family in the town from which his family originated. Joseph was of the line of David, so we had to go to David's city – Bethlehem.

Joseph and I were anxious. The journey would be long, particularly as we would need to avoid the dangers of hostile Samaria. For additional safety, we decided to travel with others making the same journey. Once Joseph had managed to find a donkey for me to ride, we set off.

God protected us. We arrived in Bethlehem about a week after leaving home. It was evening and we were travel-weary. 'We'll never find a room,' I fretted. Bethlehem was packed with visitors registering for the census.

Joseph knocked on the doors of several homes, but their guest rooms were all full. We tried to trust that God would care for us, but we couldn't help worrying. Finally, our prayers were answered. 'The only space I have is where the animals sleep,' apologised a kindly householder, looking pityingly at me. 'You are welcome to stay there. It will be warm, and I changed the straw this morning.'

And so my first child, the Son of God, was
born amongst the cattle. It was frightening. I
was young and far from home. I longed for my
mother, but our host's kind wife helped me. As
soon as I heard my son's first cry and held my
beautiful boy in my arms, I forgot the fear and
pain and wept with joy. I fed him and wrapped

him tightly in strips of cloth to keep him secure and warm. When Joseph finally persuaded me that I needed to sleep, I laid Jesus in a manger, the frame that held the animals' hay.

In the small hours of the morning, Joseph gently woke me. I thought my baby must need feeding, but through my bleary eyes I saw that he was sleeping peacefully. 'What is it?' I asked Joseph.

'We have visitors.'

I looked up to see three men, dressed in the warm, rough clothes of shepherds. 'Shalom,' they greeted me. 'We're sorry to disturb your sleep, but we must greet the saviour.' Looking a little embarrassed, one of them explained, 'An angel came to us while we were watching over our sheep.' When I told him that I recognised his description of the angel he continued with greater confidence. 'We were terrified,' he admitted, 'but the angel said that he brought great news.'

Another shepherd took over the tale. 'The
angel told us that a baby had just been born
in Bethlehem. He said the baby would be a
saviour.'

'He said we would find him lying in a
manger,' smiled the first shepherd, looking
over at Jesus. Then he turned his gaze upon me,
his eyes still dazed by what he had experienced.
'Other angels appeared, singing – lots of them.

It was beautiful. They sang, "Glory to God in the highest, and on earth peace to those who have pleased him."'

The shepherds knelt in silence next to my sleeping boy. As dawn broke, they took their leave of us. I knew that they would tell everybody they met all that had happened that night.

These events still hold a firm place in my heart and mind. I ponder them now as I pondered them then. My son. A saviour.

When Jesus was eight days old we followed Jewish custom and took him to the temple in Jerusalem to dedicate him to God and make our sacrifices. We had to pass through the city on our journey home.

When we arrived at the temple, a holy man approached us, wonder in his eyes. 'My name is Simeon,' he told me, his voice trembling with emotion. 'May I hold your baby?' With Jesus in his arms, his voice grew steady and loud. 'Sovereign Lord, you promised that I would not die before I had seen your son. You can now dismiss me in peace, for I have seen the salvation you have prepared for all people.' Simeon's words attracted attention from others. They stared as he continued, 'This child will change many things. There will be conflict. Many will speak against him.' Then, looking kindly at me, he said softly, 'And a sword will pierce your own soul too.' This made me shiver. The image was painful, but what did he mean by 'too'? How much was my son going to suffer?

A very old lady, a prophetess, tapped me on the elbow. Quietly, she answered some of

the questions in my heart. I was so young, so
innocent. I had so much to think about.

I also had a baby to care for. Any mother will
tell you how busy your first child keeps you.
Any mother will also tell you that anxiety settles
upon your soul like an uninvited guest you fear
will never leave. And most mothers haven't
been visited by angels and warned of their
child's frightening future! However, most of the
time, like all mothers, I managed to push my
fear aside and enjoy Jesus's childhood.

Jesus was a wonderful son. Of course, he
could be mischievous and playful, like any child,
but I have years of happy memories which I
often summon to comfort my old age.

Joseph and I tried to be good parents.
We taught our children the scriptures and
Jewish law. Every year, our family travelled
to Jerusalem to celebrate the Passover feast.

Although the journey was long, we made it safer and more enjoyable by travelling with friends and relatives. It was an annual family holiday.

One year, when Jesus was twelve, we lost him. Having enjoyed a wonderful Passover, Joseph and I relaxed as we and our friends left Jerusalem for the journey home. We assumed that Jesus was somewhere in the crowd of travellers. He was a sensible boy. We never worried that he would do anything silly. At the end of our first day's journey, we started to look for him. 'Sorry – haven't seen him all day,' people told us.

'We'll have to go back into the city,' said Joseph, worried. As soon as the sun rose the next morning, Joseph and I turned back. We searched everywhere except for the most obvious place. We asked everybody we saw whether they had seen a twelve-year-old boy, alone. We were growing quite frantic when a priest approached us. 'There's a boy in the temple,' he said. 'Could he be your son?'

'Of course! The temple!' How could we have failed to think of that? 'Is he well?' asked Joseph.

'Very well indeed. That's quite a boy you've got there! He understands the scriptures better than some of us who've been studying them all our lives!'

We hurried to the temple, where we found Jesus talking to a group of men on the steps. We probably embarrassed him by rushing towards him, full of the anger that accompanies a parent's relief.

He politely excused himself from the men and led us away. 'Did you not know that I must be about my father's business?' he asked, genuinely puzzled.

I feared that this might mark the turning point, when Jesus would assume the responsibilities for which he had been born. You can probably understand my relief when this didn't seem to be the case. Although he began to study the scriptures even more avidly than before, and he certainly prayed more often, he still seemed content to play with his friends and learn practical skills from Joseph. Nevertheless, there was a focus deep within him, a sense of purpose that I could never reach.

The years passed and little changed. When Jesus was in his late twenties, I noticed that he was growing restless, but still he stayed at home. I wondered whether he was waiting for a sign that his work should begin. If so, what would the sign be? Did he know?

Elizabeth and Zechariah visited us. John had left home some time ago. Elizabeth smiled fondly, but a little sadly, when she described how he had become a wandering prophet, living in the wilderness and baptising people in the River Jordan. 'They call him John the Baptist,' Zechariah added, putting his arm around Elizabeth's shoulders. Jesus listened with interest.

'Perhaps you should go to John,' I suggested to Jesus. What would have happened if I hadn't said that? Would he have gone anyway? Would he still be alive today? Would God's word have gone unheard?

Jesus was unusual. When he wanted to do something, he didn't discuss it endlessly like many people. He prayed, reached a decision, and acted upon it. That's what he did that night. Instead of sleeping, he spent the night in fervent prayer. The following morning, he announced, 'I am going to John.' After a brief farewell, he left.

I suppose that was the day I lost my son. It was a painful parting for me. When Jesus did eventually return to Nazareth, he was a changed man. No longer the son I had known, I suppose he was his true self – God's son. Explaining to me the significance of his baptism by John, he said, 'I have come to bring people back to God. That day with John was the beginning of my mission.'

In Jesus's absence, I kept myself busy with the usual duties of a wife and mother, but he was always in my mind. Eventually, we heard news that he and a group of men were travelling from village to village, teaching people to love

God and to love each other. When I enquired about their welfare, I learned that they had nothing; that they relied on people's generosity for food and shelter. Although I felt a mother's concern, I trusted Jesus's judgement.

Before long, Nazareth was buzzing with talk about Jesus. 'He heals the sick,' one neighbour told me. 'Yes, I heard that he made a blind person see,' added another. I even heard that he had made lame people walk, and had restored dead people to life. Some thought he had lost his mind, but I didn't doubt any of the things I heard.

Jesus and his friends were using a house in Capernaum, on the shore of the Sea of Galilee, as a base. Even though Capernaum was only a day's walk from Nazareth, many months passed before Jesus returned and introduced us to his friends. I liked them all – especially Simon. A fisherman by trade, he was a hard-working man who seemed devoted to Jesus. It reassured me to know that Jesus had such a man amongst his friends.

When Jesus did eventually return to Nazareth he came to teach rather than to visit. People were bursting with curiosity, and the synagogue was bursting at the seams.

Jesus was spellbinding. You might smile to hear me speak so fondly, but it is true. As he read the words of the Prophet Isaiah, we listened in awed silence. 'The spirit of the Lord is upon me,' he read. 'He has anointed me to bring good news to the poor. He has sent me to proclaim freedom for prisoners and sight for the blind, to release the oppressed.' I remember the light in Jesus's eyes. 'Today this scripture is fulfilled in your hearing.' There were surprised gasps; people looked at him in admiration. I also heard a low murmur amongst some. 'Isn't he just Mary's son?'

'You probably want me to heal people here, in my home town, just as you have heard that I did in Capernaum,' Jesus said to them. Many nodded. His reply disappointed them. 'People in other villages didn't know who I was, so they needed signs. But you have known me all my life. You should understand my words.'

The murmuring I had noticed earlier grew louder, the words more distinct. 'Is he saying that he won't help us? Are there no miracles for us in Nazareth?' Men rose to their feet, moving threateningly towards Jesus.

I watched in horror as burly men bustled Jesus out of the

synagogue. They pushed him towards the edge
of the cliff on which Nazareth is built. Terrified,
I caught at people's clothes, begging and pleading
with them to spare him.

'Shove him over the edge,' someone shouted.

They had Jesus right at the edge of a cliff.
I held my breath, but Jesus was unafraid. He
looked them in the eye, moved their hands aside,
and passed back through the crowd. As he reached
the safety of the village he turned back to them and
said, 'No prophet is accepted in his home town.'

I was deeply shaken. Did he meet such hostility
everywhere he went?

Jesus's work brought him in our direction only
a few more times, when he would fill our small
house with his friends. I understood why people
were so drawn to him; he was a wonderful person
to be with. When he talked with you, he gave you
his full attention, as though his mind was empty

of everything but you. This wasn't just with me, his mother; he did this with everybody, whether old friends or strangers. Do you think that is a sign of perfect love?

Occasionally I managed to join Jesus for a few days, but I felt overwhelmed by the crowds. His teaching was simple: we should love God, and we should love each other as God loves us.

Jesus understood the way people thought. He could see the gaps in their commitment to God, the obstacles that stood in their way, and he was not afraid to bring them to people's attention. For most people, this was helpful. They went away with a new sense of purpose. However, there are always those who are resistant to the truth – particularly if it is an unwelcome truth about themselves. I saw with concern that he sometimes made enemies.

Some of these enemies were powerful men – our religious leaders, the Pharisees. They taught strict observance of the law, whereas Jesus taught that people should apply the law with love and compassion. He argued that the Pharisees sometimes forgot the loving intention of God's law. The Sadducees were even more powerful. They were the temple priests, often used by the Romans to uphold their laws. We look up to our religious leaders, having been taught this respect since childhood, and they have power over most aspects of our lives. Jesus argued that this power was being abused, that many of our leaders had become corrupt.

However, Jesus also continued to make many friends. He once introduced me to a group of wealthy women who, he said, provided enough financial support to make his work possible. One of them was Joanne, the wealthy wife of King Herod's steward. Another, Mary Magdalene, explained how she had met Jesus. 'He healed me,' she said simply. 'He drove out the dark demons of my life and showed me the light.'

I felt the interest that any mother would feel when her single, thirty-one-year-old son introduces a beautiful young woman. In hindsight, I can see that this rose from my weakness, a desire for my son to be safe, to be a family man. Jesus was so committed to his work that I doubt whether marriage ever crossed his mind. I also suspect that he knew that his life would be short.

When I look back, I realise that Jesus loved all of humanity equally, whether friends, enemies, or even family. As his family, we sometimes found this painful. Once, having not seen him for several months, we heard that he was preaching nearby. Jesus's brothers and I hurried to see him. 'Can you tell Jesus that we are here?' we eagerly asked a friend we recognised. I was later told that, upon hearing the message, Jesus had replied, 'Who is my mother?

My mother and brothers are those who hear God's words and put them into practice.' I understood that Jesus wasn't just mine any more. What Simeon had said was true. It felt as though a sword was piercing my heart.

There then followed a difficult time for us. Joseph suffered a long illness, his slow decline keeping us at home. I was still mourning his death when we heard the terrible news that Elizabeth's son John had been executed by King Herod. John had criticised Herod for marrying his brother's widow. I visited Elizabeth and we tried to console each other in our grief. I grew increasingly anxious for my own son in a dangerous world.

News of miraculous events continued to reach us. One story was that Jesus had fed five thousand people with just two fish and five loaves of bread. His healing ministry continued. As the revitalisation of our religion gathered pace, Jesus needed more help. He chose about seventy of his followers to travel the region preaching and healing. It was said that they, like Jesus, could cast out demons and heal the sick.

As you grow older, the years seem to pass more quickly. Passover seemed to come round sooner every year. The year after Joseph died I looked forward to it with less excitement than usual. It would be the first time I had travelled to Jerusalem without him. I planned to travel with my children and friends as usual. Mary Magdalene kindly helped me to cover the costs.

I hoped to meet Jesus in Jerusalem. He had been moving slowly in that direction for some time, continuing his ministry as he went.

Just after entering the city walls, I found myself chatting to somebody who had recently seen Jesus in Jericho. He described to me how people had lined the streets, trying to catch a glimpse of him. 'A tax collector called Zaccheus climbed a tree to see over the heads of those in front,' he laughed. I smiled as I listened. 'Jesus called out to Zaccheus that he wanted to stay in his house. Zaccheus almost fell out of the tree in astonishment.' I giggled. I knew that Jesus would have been pleased. Most people hate tax collectors, because they are usually corrupt. Jesus had shown the crowd what forgiveness means. Another man forgiven and accepted by God.

Our conversation was interrupted by a crescendo of noise. Men, women and children were running into the street, shouting, tearing down palm branches and laying them on the road. In the distance I could hear voices singing psalms of hope and praise. The singing came nearer. What was happening? The palm is our national emblem, so this felt like the beginning of an uprising, or at least a protest against Roman rule. I felt a terrible sense of foreboding.

'He's coming!' I heard somebody shout. Standing on my tiptoes, trying to see over people's heads, I was just able to catch a glimpse of a man riding a donkey into the city. It was exactly as the scriptures had promised. My sense of dread became more specific. My heart missed a beat. It was Jesus. As my son passed through the crowds, people joined the procession, which grew larger and louder. Never before had I experienced such crowds; never before had I experienced such emotion, either in myself or in others.

I noticed some Pharisees looking very anxious by the roadside. Were they concerned for their own positions, or were they concerned for all of these innocent people, daring to oppose the great might of Rome? I felt compelled to follow as Jesus led the crowd to the temple.

Reaching the temple court, Jesus stopped. The crowd stopped, holding its collective breath. For the first time in my life, I saw anger in my son's face. What was wrong? What would he do? 'This is it!' whispered a man to my left. 'This is the beginning of our freedom!' He must have been bitterly disappointed when, mastering his anger, Jesus gently dispersed the crowd.

The next morning I was near the temple when Jesus returned, his face firm with resolution. The scene greeting him was the same as the previous day. Money-lenders and tradesmen carried out their business of exploitation and corruption within the temple. Jesus and his friends marched in and caused chaos, overturning the tables of

the money-lenders and releasing sacrificial
animals. Jesus angrily accused people of
abusing God's house. More enemies. It was
now only a matter of time.

Jesus was busy, and I spent only an hour with
him on the afternoon of the Passover. When
the time came to say farewell, he held me tight.
It felt like goodbye. I went back to my lodging
and wept, waiting for news.
The next day, Simon
came to see me, deeply
troubled. He told me
everything that had
happened the
previous night. He
said that Judas, one
of Jesus's closest
friends, had
betrayed him to

the authorities. Jesus had been arrested. Simon wanted to spare me the details of the flogging Jesus had suffered, but I felt strong. Nevertheless, the description sickened me. I trembled to think of my beloved son alone in the hands of those who hated him. How could they hurt a man who taught only love and peace?

'Where are the others?' I asked Simon.

'In Bethany.'

'Are they safe?'

'I think so.'

'What will happen now?' I dreaded the answer.

Simon held my hand. 'This morning they brought Jesus before Pilate, the Roman prefect. I think Pilate recognised Jesus as a good man. He gave the crowd the opportunity to save him, but the priests had whipped the people into a frenzy. They were almost hysterical.'

'So they didn't save him?' I held my breath.

'No.' He looked away from me. 'They're going to crucify him. Today.'

I felt sick. I remembered the words of the holy man who had held Jesus as a baby: 'A sword will pierce your own soul.' I wanted to scream.

'Mary?' Simon was concerned.

I answered through my tears. 'Leave me now. I must pray.'

Alone, I knelt and begged God to save my son, to save his own son. At first I was desperate, but I gradually felt God's calming presence. This was the responsibility for which my son had been born. For some reason, I alone amongst women had been chosen to bear this agony. I felt the hand of God on my shoulder, reassuring me that I was strong enough. I had to be strong. I could do this. I knew I had to go to my son.

'Simon!'

He came back in, this time accompanied by John, another of Jesus's friends. John wore a hood pulled low over his face. 'John will take you to the Antonine fortress,' explained Simon. 'They will probably take Jesus from there to Golgotha.' Golgotha – the place of the skulls.

We didn't reach the fortress. It was too difficult to push our way through the crowds lining the streets. Some people wept, others were exulting. All fell silent as Jesus approached.

John held me tightly. Bleeding and bruised,

Jesus was dressed in an expensive robe which was now stained with his blood. He was only thirty-three, but he was bent like an old man under the weight of the beam of his cross, which he was forced to carry. I tried to catch his attention, but though he did not meet my eye I am sure that he felt my presence. I saw Mary Magdalene and some of her friends in the crowd following Jesus.

Exhausted, Jesus stumbled, and once fell hard onto the ground. A guard lifted him roughly to his feet, then seized a man from the crowd. 'You carry his cross for him,' he growled. I heard Jesus ask the man's name as they

shouldered the cross together. 'Simon,' answered the man. 'I'm from Cyrene.'

'Thank you, Simon,' said Jesus. I wanted to thank him too.

Simon's help restored Jesus a little. He found the strength to turn to the group of weeping women following him. 'Do not weep for me,' he said, 'weep for yourselves and for your children. The time will come when you will wish you had never had children, for if people can do these things, what more are they capable of?'

At Golgotha, soldiers took the beam and fixed it across an olive trunk. When they hammered the nails into my son's wrists and ankles I felt every blow as if it were my own flesh. It was the darkest time I have ever known.

Jesus spent his last hours on a cross between two criminals who were also being crucified. A mocking notice nailed above his head read, 'This is the King of the Jews.' People in the crowd at his feet taunted him, 'If you are God's chosen one, why don't you save yourself?'

Even in his extreme suffering, Jesus found it in his heart to pray for others. Looking down at those who had gambled over the clothes of which he had been stripped before being hung on the cross, he called out, 'Father forgive them, for they do not know what they are doing.'

One of the criminals dying beside Jesus shouted angrily, 'Aren't you the Christ? Save

yourself and us!' It was difficult for the dying men
to talk. Hanging from their arms restricted their
breathing and they could only gasp enough air to
talk by lifting themselves on their nailed feet. The
man on the other side of Jesus argued against the
first. 'Don't you fear God, even now? You and I are
punished justly, but this man Jesus has done no
wrong.' Looking to Jesus, he pleaded, 'Remember
me when you come into your kingdom.'

Jesus answered him, 'Today you will be with me
in Paradise.'

I watched the life ebb from my son. Summoning his final strength, he pushed upwards on his feet and called out, 'Father, into your hands I commit my spirit.' They say the curtain in the temple tore in two at that moment. My son was dead. The world was as dark as night. The centurion in charge of the executions fell to his knees, exclaiming 'Surely this was a righteous man.'

I stayed at the foot of the cross, weeping with Mary Magdalene and other women who had loved Jesus.

Does time bring comfort? Can a mother ever recover from seeing her son in such agony?

We prepared his body for burial and laid him in the tomb that one of his followers had prepared. The following day, when Mary Magdalene visited the tomb, it was empty. She returned with the amazing news that Jesus might still be alive.

This news both astonished and comforted me. Jesus's resurrection brought new life and new hope for everybody. For many years now, Jesus's followers have continued his work in the face of great dangers. The movement that Jesus founded is spreading throughout many lands. I wonder how long it will take for Jesus's vision, a world filled with love, to be realised?

I understand now that Jesus's death brings hope, not despair. He has shown us the way to God, he has forgiven us all. That is what the angel meant. That is why Jesus was born, that is why he died.

I am old now, and my story is told.

One day soon, I shall be in Paradise with my son – my saviour.

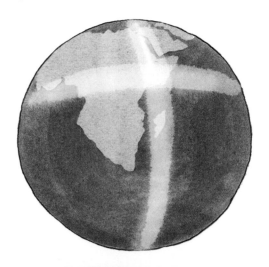

TAKING THINGS FURTHER

The real read

This *Real Reads* volume of *Mary of Galilee* is our interpretation of the events of the New Testament, told from the perspective of one of the most important participants. In writing this account of Mary's life, we have used evidence from the gospel according to Luke. This is one of the four gospels – the first four books of the New Testament.

It is important to acknowledge that all four gospels were written after Jesus's death, and that the writers had different aims in mind – although they all wanted to engender faith in the reader that Jesus was the Son of God. The first three gospels – Matthew, Mark and Luke – are called 'the synoptic gospels'. They were probably written between forty and sixty years after the crucifixion. The gospel according to John, written later, is significantly different.

Sometimes the four gospels' accounts of events differ considerably. At first this made our task rather difficult, until we realised that what we needed to do was present the New Testament as it is, rather than to weave a path of our choice between the gospels. Therefore, if you read all six books in the *Real Reads* New Testament series, you may well notice some of the apparent contradictions and inconsistencies that are present in the Bible itself.

In writing each of the six *Real Reads* New Testament books we chose a specific source to follow. To write Mary's account we chose Luke's gospel because it gives far more information about Mary and about the birth of Jesus than any of the other gospels. However, most people's understanding of the nativity is a combination of Luke and Matthew. Luke does not mention the visit of the wise men, or even the flight from King Herod. It is generally accepted that these were added to the birth story at a later date and for a particular purpose. As we have followed Luke's account, the wise men do not appear in the *Real Reads* version.

As far as we are aware, Mary did not record her

thoughts and experiences, so we do not know what she thought of the events through which she lived. Using thorough research and paying close attention to the Bible account, we have tried to imagine what she might have been like, and what she might have thought.

It is quite probable that Mary played a role in the development of the Christian church after Jesus's death. As his mother, she would almost certainly have visited his tomb. In Luke, we read that Mary Magdalene was in the company of other women at the tomb, but it does not specify Jesus's mother. We therefore made the decision not to include this in the *Real Reads Mary of Galilee*.

This version of Mary's story does not cover all the events of the New Testament. Reading the other five books in the series will bring you closer to an understanding of the complete story. You may then want to read the New Testament itself. We recommend that you read either the *New International Version* or *The Youth Bible*, details of which are given below.

Biblical sources

Although *Mary of Galilee* is based on the story as told in the gospel of Luke, there are places where we have drawn on other sources. On the *Real Reads* website you will find an online concordance (www.realreads.co.uk/newtestament/ concordance/maryofgalilee). A 'bible concordance' is an indexing tool which allows you to see how the same words, sentences and passages appear in different versions and translations of the Bible. This online concordance will direct you from events in the *Real Reads* version back to their biblical sources, so you can see clearly where each part of our story is drawn from.

Life in
New Testament times

The main events of Mary's life took place in Palestine, a long narrow area of land bordered to the west by the Mediterranean Sea and to the east by the Transjordanian Desert. Some parts of Palestine were desert, some were hill country, some rich pasture land, and some uncultivated wilderness.

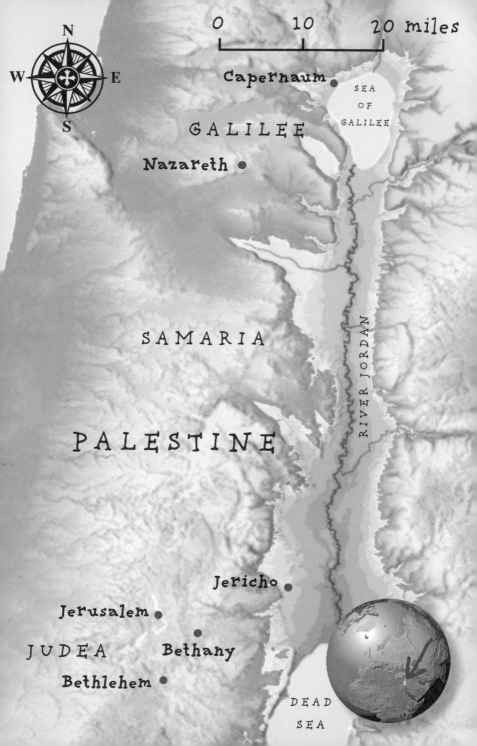

Although Palestine was Jewish land, it was part of the Roman Empire and under Roman control. The Jews resented paying taxes to Rome. During Jesus's lifetime, there was considerable conflict between the Jews and their Roman rulers. This helps to explain why the Romans might have been nervous of the crowds following Jesus.

The Jews considered Palestine to be their 'promised land', promised to them by God. Moses had led them there from slavery in Egypt. The area was mainly Jewish, with synagogues and temples. Nevertheless, it is interesting that most of Jesus's ministry took place around the Sea of Galilee, an area with a mixed population of Jews and Gentiles, and a reputation for political unrest.

Nazareth, where Jesus is commonly believed to have grown up, was a rather insignificant town – some argue that it did not even exist at that time. Mary and her family were probably quite poor. Although it is common belief that Joseph was a carpenter, it is more likely that he worked with stone than with wood. Most people lived in very basic houses built of mud or stone, often sharing part of their home with their animals.

The routines of life followed the seasons as many people were involved in agriculture. Most would have kept goats and sheep. The area was fertile, growing a range of fruit, grain and vegetables. Fish and bread were staples of their diet.

Jews of the time, as is still the case for many orthodox Jews today, followed very strict laws. The Old Testament tells the story of how these laws, the Torah, were handed down from God to Moses. Mary, Joseph and Jesus would all have had detailed knowledge of the Torah.

Finding out more

We recommend the following books and websites to gain a greater understanding of the New Testament.

Books

We strongly recommend that you read the rest of the *Real Reads New Testament* series, as the six narratives interlock to give a more complete picture of events. These are *Jesus of Nazareth*, *Simon Peter*, *Judas Iscariot*, *Mary Magdalene* and *Paul of Tarsus*.

- *New Century Youth Bible*, Authentic Lifestyle, 2007.

- *Mary: The Mother of Jesus*, Tomie dePaola Holiday House, 1995.

- *Just Like Mary*, Rosemarie Gortler and Donna Piscitelli, Our Sunday Visitor, 2003.

- W. B. Yeats, *Mother of God*. A short poem, to be found in most Yeats anthologies.

Websites

- www.bibleplaces.com
Particularly interesting discussion and pictures relating to Bethlehem.

- www.localhistories.org/new.html
Brief but useful descriptions of many aspects of everyday life in New Testament times.

- www.bbc.co.uk/religion/religions/ christianity/history/virginmary
Interesting information and discussion.

TV and film

- *Jesus of Nazareth*, directed by Franco Zeffirelli, ITV DVD, 1977. A six and a half hour mini-series.

- *Nativity Story*, directed by Catherine Hardwicke, Entertainment in Video, 2007.

- *Silent Night: The story of the First Nativity*, Abbey Home Media, 2004. A short, lively animation, which includes the wise men and Herod.

Food for thought

Here are some things to think about if you are reading *Mary of Galilee* alone, or ideas for discussion if you are reading it with friends.

Starting points

- What differences do you notice between this version of Jesus's birth and the story with which you are probably more familiar?

- What role do angels play in Mary's story? How do you imagine it would be to be visited by an angel? What messages do you think angels might bring to the world today?

- Why might it be important for Christians that Jesus was born to a poor family?

- Can you tell the story of the night of Jesus's birth from the viewpoint of one of the shepherds?

- Can you find examples of times when Mary fears for Jesus's safety?

- When Mary looks back on Jesus's life, what do you think she understands about his death?

- Why do you think Mary is such an important person for many Christians?

Group activities

- With a group of friends, act out this version of the birth of Jesus. Stop at different points and interview Mary and Joseph about how they feel.

- As a group, find all the evidence you can that Mary was a loving mother to Jesus.

- Choose four important events from the story, taking it in turns to play the part of Mary. After each scene, interview the person playing Mary about their experience and feelings. You could turn these interviews into an interesting newspaper-style report.